I0799190

SPOT

AROUND TOWN

DOCTOR'S OFFICE

by Susan Rose Simms

amicus LEARNING

scale

nurse

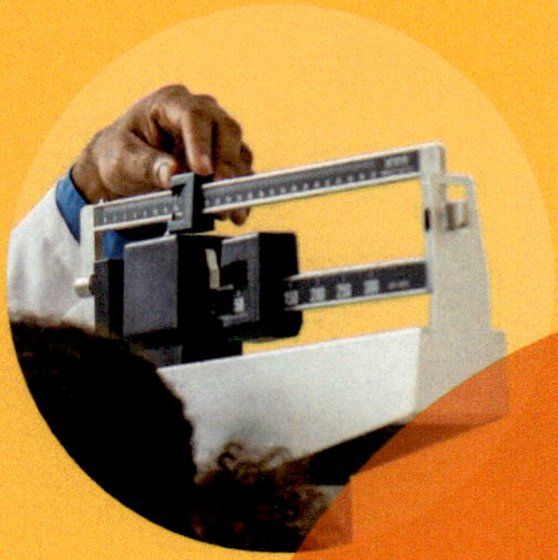

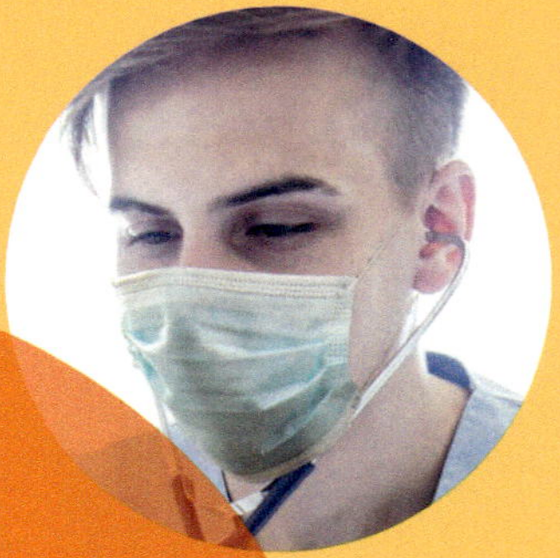

Look for these words and pictures as you read.

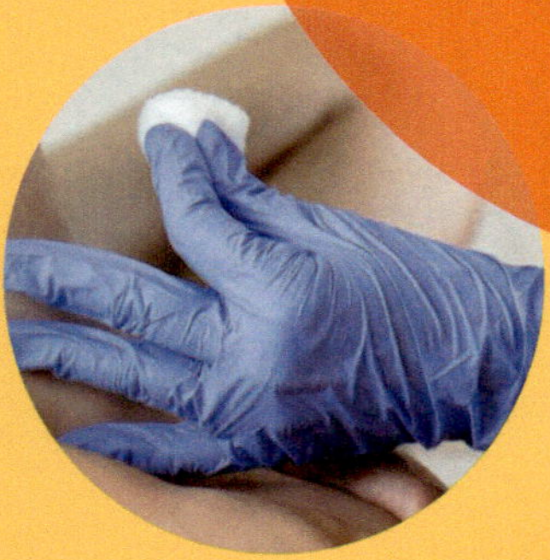

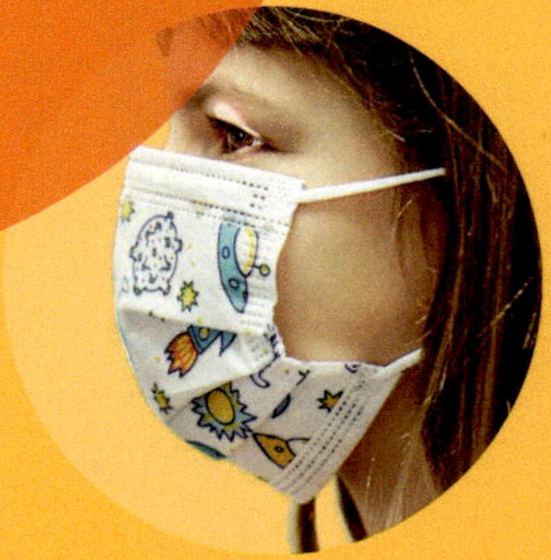

gloves

mask

Let's go to the doctor's office. What will we see?

MALA PRIVREDA U JUGOSLAVIJI

Look at the waiting room.
People wait for their turn.

Look at the scale.
It shows your weight.

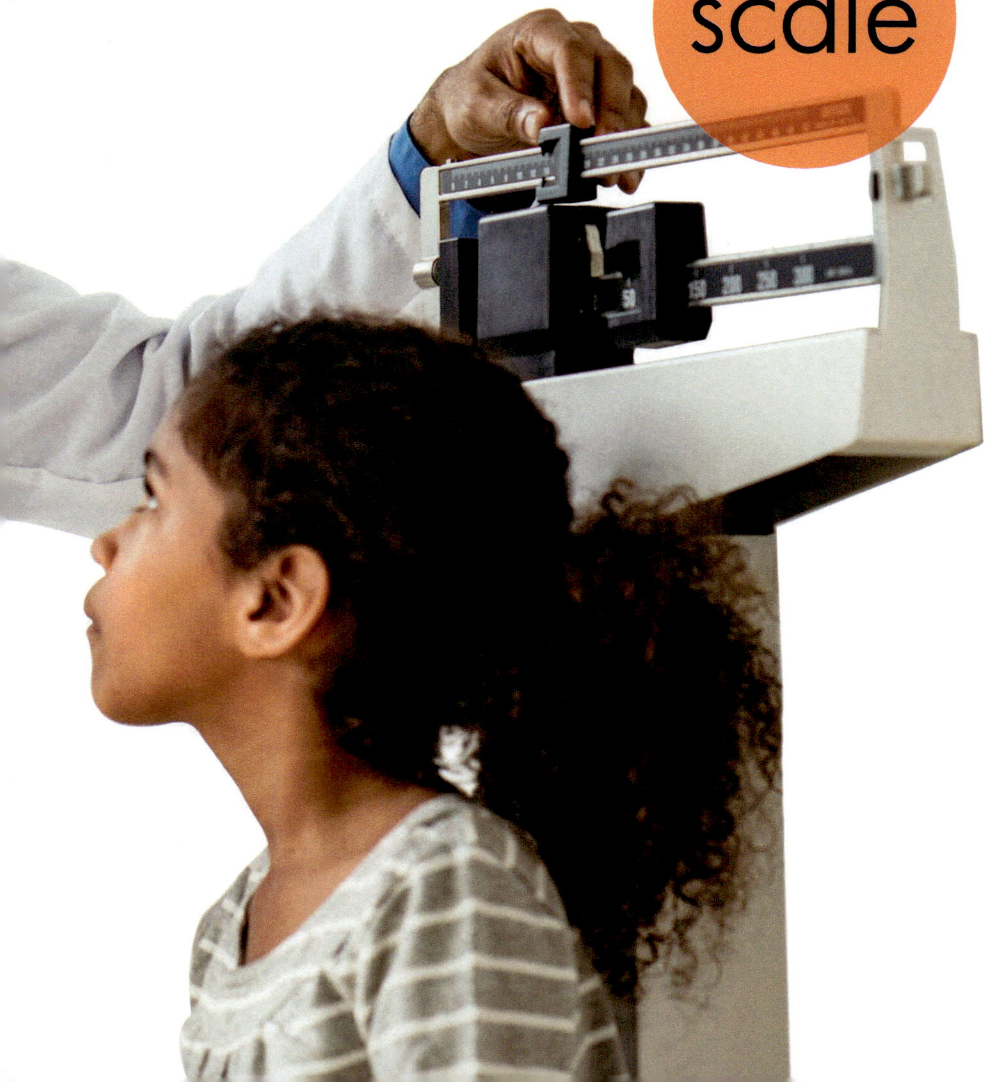

Look at the nurse.
He helps the doctor.
He checks Nora's heart.

nurse

Look at the gloves.
The doctor wears them.
They keep things clean.

gloves

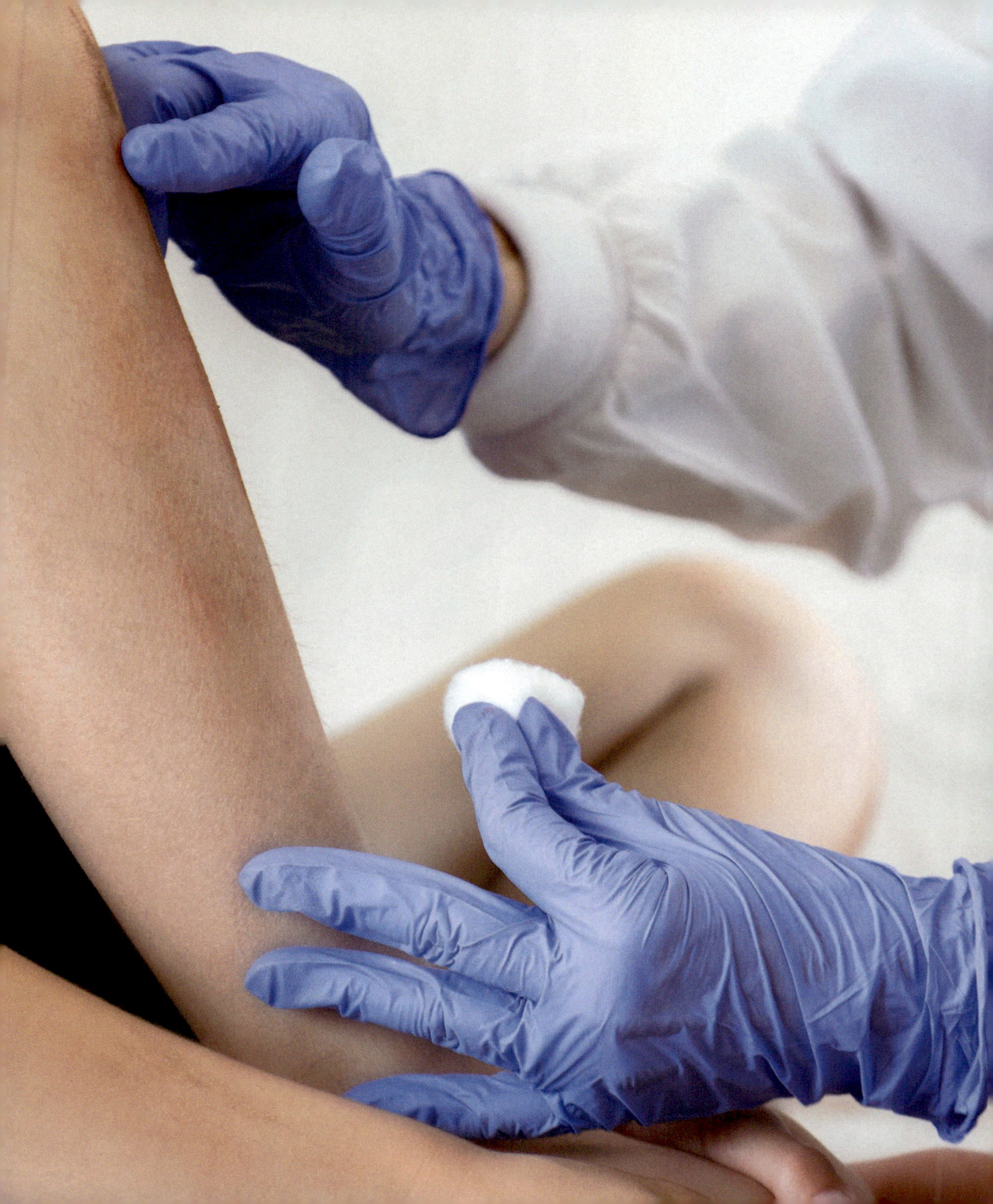

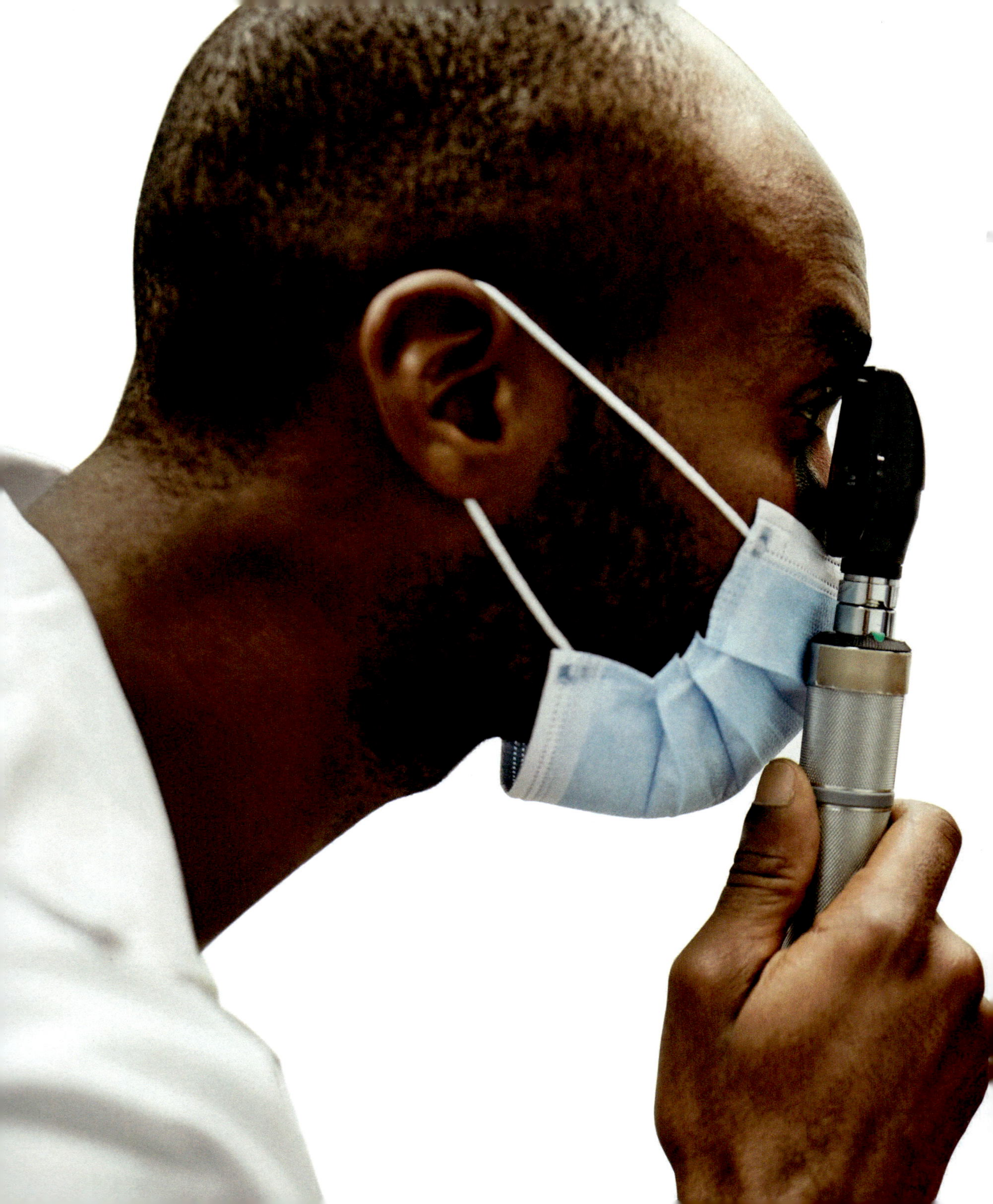

mask

Look at the mask.
It keeps the germs away.

The office closes for the night. The doctor will help more people tomorrow.

scale

nurse

Did you find?

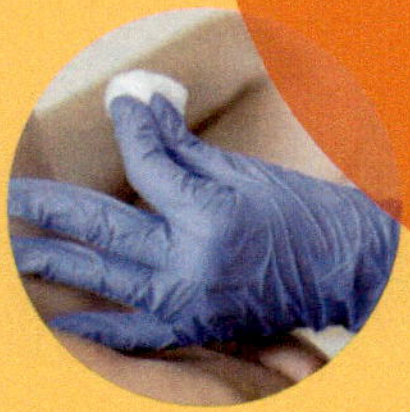

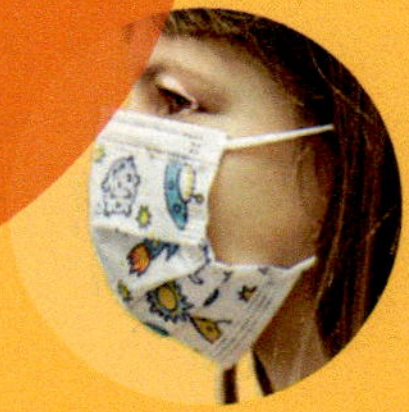

gloves

mask

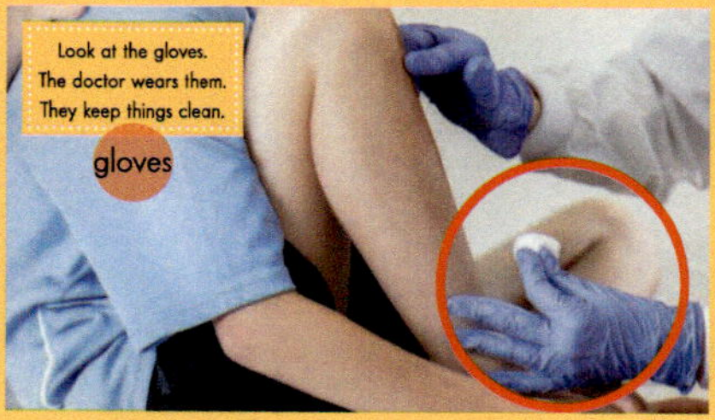

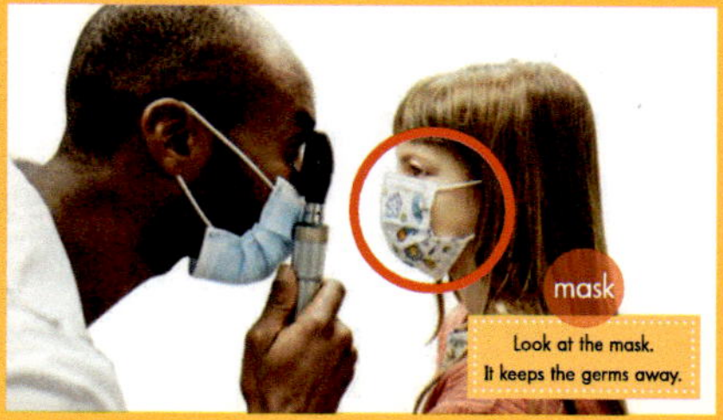

SPOT

Spot is published by Amicus Learning, an imprint of Amicus
P.O. Box 227, Mankato, MN 56002
www.amicuspublishing.us

Copyright © 2026 Amicus.
International copyright reserved in all countries.
No part of this book may be reproduced in any form without written permission from the publisher.

Names: Simms, Susan Rose author
Title: Doctor's office / by: Susan Rose Simms.
Description: Mankato, MN : Amicus Learning, an imprint of Amicus, [2026] | Series: Spot around town | Audience: Ages 4–7 | Audience: Grades K–1 | Summary: "What do people see at the doctor's office? From the lobby to an X-ray, this low-level beginning reader reinforces new vocabulary with a search-and-find feature. A great early social studies book to inspire learning about communities on field trips for kindergartners and first graders"— Provided by publisher.
Identifiers: LCCN 2025012847 (print) | LCCN 2025012848 (ebook) | ISBN 9798892008259 library binding | ISBN 9798892008914 paperback | ISBN 9798892009577 ebook
Subjects: LCSH: Medical care—Juvenile literature | Medical offices—Juvenile literature | Children—Preparation for medical care—Juvenile literature
Classification: LCC R130.5 .S536 2026 (print) | LCC R130.5 (ebook) | DDC 610—dc23/eng/20250721
LC record available at https://lccn.loc.gov/2025012847
LC ebook record available at https:/lccn.loc.gov/2025012848

Printed in United States of America

Ana Brauer, editor
Deb Miner, series designer
Sara Hood, book designer and photo researcher

Photos by Getty Images/FG Trade, 3, Hispanolistic, 2, 8–9, 15, Morsa Images, 2, 12–13, 15, SDI Productions, 2, 10–11, 15, South_agency, 4–5, Tetra Images, 2, 6–7, 15; Shutterstock/ Angelina Avei, 1, DC Studio, cover, 16, oneinchpunch, 14